Alabama Miracles

*Real life stories
to warm the heart
and lift the spirit*

Lynn Grisard Fullman

Seacoast Publishing
Birmingham, Alabama

Lynn Grisard Fullman

ISBN 1-878561-24-3

Published by
Seacoast Publishing Inc.
110 12th St. North
Birmingham, Ala. 35203
(205) 250-8016

Cover design by Lori Leath Smith
Cover photo copyright © 1994 Jeff Greenberg

Manufactured in the United States

Contents

The miracles

Dedication

To find someone to believe in you is a miracle.

To find someone to teach you about miracles may be a greater one.

This book is dedicated to the two people who have done both, my parents, Margaret Conner Grisard and James Lindsay Grisard Sr., who live in Chattanooga, Tenn.

Without them, I would not be here—and I would not have learned about miracles.

They are the best—and I love them both.

Foreword

The more I have talked with Alabamians about their miracles and messages, the more convinced I have become that a power beyond our understanding is among us.

How else could a clump of daisies grow overnight to assure someone that a message had been received and understood?

Who hollered someone's name just in time to divert disaster?

How could a child be pulled—by an unseen stranger—from the depths of a swimming pool where he had lain dead?

Why would a perfect stranger stop to give an answer to a question he had not known?

What power could make a woman walk again

after years in a wheelchair?

If there were no such thing as miracles, how could these things have happened?

Many of the stories recounted here have never before been told. But, they came together, because—by a miracle—people felt led to share their tidings of comfort and joy.

I have been touched by their telling, and I trust that others will be, too.

After collecting these stories of miracles and messages delivered in Alabama, I am more convinced than ever that, indeed, we do not live alone.

Someone who cares about us very much walks with us, sharing our journey, holding our hands.

If ever you have thought you were alone, these stories may convince you otherwise.

—*Lynn Grisard Fullman*

Alabama Miracles

Lynn Grisard Fullman

Lynn Grisard Fullman

The daisies

Virginia Rainey
Greenville, Alabama

Barbara Kiningham was only in her 30s when she was diagnosed with cancer.

A determined woman, with three small children, Barbara refused to let the threat of cancer get her down.

"I'm going to beat this," she promised.

But, beating it did not mean staying on earth. It meant, after a two-year battle, that Barbara died.

Barbara's friend in Chattanooga, Haven Conner, was troubled by the death. Not because Barbara had gone on to a better life, but because the two, long-time friends had not had time to mend a disagreement.

Haven and Barbara had met in college at Samford University in Birmingham, had been sorority sisters, had lived together after college. Later, after both married, they talked every day.

For years, the two shared most everything. Before Barbara's marriage, together the friends had chosen her silverware pattern which was a pattern with daisies. Daisies were Barbara's favorite flowers.

Barbara had carried daisies in her bridal bouquet and Haven had carried them as she served as a bridesmaid.

A dozen years into their special relationship, a disagreement divided their friendship.

The two quit sharing birthdays, stopped talking daily, quit laughing and crying together.

Although Haven had heard Barbara had been sick, she was not prepared for her death.

In the years that followed Barbara's death, Haven never quit agonizing over what had been left unsaid. She had assumed that, in time, there would be the chance to work things out.

Barbara was on Haven's mind one day as she mowed her lawn.

Hot and tired, Haven went inside and slumped into a chair.

With her family away and the house quiet, Haven began pouring out her regrets and hurts to Barbara.

A strong Christian and spiritual person, Barbara seemed almost to be there. Out loud, Haven told her how guilty she had felt about what had happened between them, and she asked for Barbara's understanding and forgiveness.

After 30 minutes, having said everything that had been buried in her heart since Barbara's death, Haven asked for a sign that Barbara had heard and had understood.

The next morning, in the middle of the yard that had just been cut, there stood a foot-high clump of flowers.

They were daisies.

Lynn Grisard Fullman

The woman at the pool

Angela and Andrew Welch
Greenville, Alabama

"Is this Mrs. William Andrew Welch?" the voice on the telephone asked.

'Yes, it is," answered the Greenville resident.

"Hold the line, please," the polite voice continued.

Before Mrs. Welch had time to consider who might be calling, she heard someone crying, sobbing and an occasional word, "Andrew. Andrew."

Fear gripped Mrs. Welch.

"What is it," she demanded, thinking of her

five-year-old son, Andrew, who was in Birmingham visiting her sister.

"Who is this? What are you trying to say," Mrs. Welch implored.

The caller continued incoherently.

"Andrew. Andrew. Andrew. Andrew drowned."

Then, more sobbing.

Finally recognizing her sister's voice, Mrs. Welch demanded to talk with someone who could tell her what was happening.

A nurse took the phone and explained.

Andrew had been at a Birmingham area country club with his aunt when he went into the swimming pool without his water wings.

Nobody noticed when the youngster slipped into the water, or his struggling to get back to the side.

No one saw when little Andrew drifted to the bottom of the pool.

Finally, someone did notice and a life-guard began to administer mouth-to-mouth resuscitation.

Paramedics were called, and they confirmed there were no vital signs. For several long minutes, the boy had been without life.

By the time Andrew was taken to The Children's Hospital of Alabama, he was showing some signs of life.

When the call was placed to his parents, the child had been taken to X-Ray.

"We're on the way," Mrs. Welch screamed into

the phone as she raced out the door for the 120-mile drive to Birmingham.

The couple, both involved in the medical profession, expected the worst when they arrived in Birmingham.

The worst, though, was not what they found.

The couple found Andrew in intensive care where he was eating mashed potatoes and fried chicken.

He smiled at his parents who had burned up the motor in their car to reach Birmingham in just more than an hour.

There was not a dry eye anywhere, as people hugged and cried and tried to understand what had happened that July day in 1983.

In intensive care, where he remained until doctors were convinced he had no damage of any sort, a wide-eyed Andrew asked his mother, "Mommy, did I die?"

"Yes," she told him as tears streamed down her face.

The rest of what happened she would not know until later.

It took the youngster three years to piece together the events of that day. When he did, he told his mother what he remembered.

Andrew told his mother that as he was getting into the pool, a woman, reading a book, looked up from her chair to warn him, "Be careful. You might get hurt."

Once in the water and unable to swim, Andrew

Lynn Grisard Fullman

remembered trying to swim to the side of the pool. He remembered seeing people's legs under water. He could see, but not reach, the ladder on the side of the pool.

He remembered struggling to the side until, exhausted, he let his arms fall to the sides of his body as he slipped to the bottom.

Suddenly, someone jerked him from the water.

The woman, who had warned Andrew to be careful, came for him, lifted him out of the water and onto the side of the pool.

Andrew's aunt, seeing his blue and lifeless body, became hysterical and fainted. The woman who had pulled Andrew to safety scooped up the aunt's two preschoolers, took the children to their own home and left them there with the maid.

To this day, no one remembers having seen the woman. Outsiders are not allowed at the club unless they are accompanied by a member. But, a check of sign-in records at the country club gave no clue to the woman's identity. She was not a member, nor had she registered with a member.

No one who was there that day knows who the woman could have been. Nor do they know how she managed to take the two children to their home, how she plunged unnoticed into the pool to pull Andrew from the bottom.

But, Andrew knows, without a doubt, that it was she who snatched him from the depths.

Dreams to be feared

Sheila Beasley
Tuscaloosa, Alabama

After Sheila Beasley's parents' home near Demopolis had burned, her life never again has been quite the same.

Although the damage caused by the ravages of the fire could be repaired, something about that incident lingered in Sheila's mind.

Every time Sheila dreamed about the fire, someone she knew died the next day.

The first time she dreamed about the fire, she dreamed also about the impending wedding ceremony that her Uncle Thurston had agreed to perform for the Beasleys. (The couple, who originally had been married in a civil ceremony, had asked him to do a Christian service as they renewed their vows.)

In the dream, Sheila was upstairs, waiting for the ceremony to begin.

As her grandmother urged her to hurry, Sheila smelled flowers and heard wedding music floating up from downstairs.

"I'll be down in a minute," Sheila told her grandmother.

Sheila dreamed that she kept wanting to go downstairs, but just couldn't walk.

Before Sheila could finish her dream, her alarm clock startled her back to reality.

Later that day, Sheila got the news. Her Uncle Thurston, who lived in Warrior, had died of a massive heart attack.

Another time, the house-burning dream forewarned more bad news.

In that dream, lots of children were in her parents' home when the sky turned black and rains dumped from the sky.

In her dream, Sheila watched as the children sought shelter in the workshop behind the house. Running hysterically, over and over they screamed, "It's a tornado. We're going to die. We're going to die."

The next day, Sheila heard that a boy she had grown up with had been killed in a traffic accident.

The wreck had happened in front of an elementary school.

The last time Sheila dreamed about the burning house, her dream took on a new twist.

After seeing her parents' house in flames, Sheila, in her dream, ran across the street where she found the home of her friends, John and Sharon. In reality, the house is not close to her parents' house.

Sheila pounded on the couple's door. When no one answered, Sheila, in her dream, went to the woods behind the house.

It was there that she saw a large, black dog with a red bandana around his neck.

The dog spoke to Sheila.

He said, "John is going to be all right."

When Sheila woke, she realized how silly her dream had been, yet she remembered what always happened after she had dreamed about the burning house.

All day she waited for bad news, hoping it would not come, but remembering too vividly what the dreams always had forewarned.

Later that day, she got the news she dreaded. John had been hurt on the job when a clogged chlorine line exploded in his face, forcing the caustic gas into his lungs.

Sheila rushed to the Northport hospital to be with Sharon, whose husband was injured.

As the two women waited on word from John, Sheila told Sharon about the dream, about the

Lynn Grisard Fullman

black dog wearing the bandana—and the message the dog had given her.

A strange look crossed Sharon's face as she heard the story.

Just before the doctors came to assure Sharon that John would be all right, she explained something to Sheila.

John used to have a black dog.

His name was Bandana.

(Author's note: John and Sharon are fictitious names.)

One for the history books

Shirlene Gee
Talladega, Alabama

Shirlene Gee's pastor, Reverend Ralph Abernathy, asked her to write a history of their church, Sulphur Springs Baptist.

Shirlene's roots in the church ran as deeply as the church's roots dug into the Alabama community where it had been founded before the turn of the century.

It was the Lincoln church where Shirlene had grown up, where her family attended, where her grandfather, Josh Alldredge, for decades had been

Lynn Grisard Fullman

a member.

She considered how best to write a church history using the years of meeting minutes and Sunday School records.

But, the more she thought about the project, the more she decided that it was just too massive an undertaking. Maybe later, she thought, when her two preschoolers did not demand so much of her time, she would tackle the project.

Hoping someone else might take on the project, Shirlene talked with Sep Love, a commissioner with the Alabama Baptist Historical Commission.

Love explained that he was in no position to write the decades-old history. He wanted, instead, to microfilm the records, part of the Commission's ongoing undertaking to preserve Alabama Baptist history. The commission, he explained to Shirlene, would borrow, microfilm and return the church's records.

Although Shirlene was relieved to know that the records would be preserved, she still was left with the duty of writing the history.

While Shirlene pondered the history-writing project and waited for Sep to pick up the records, her father Ray Alldredge worried about the records being in her home.

"Something could happen to them," he had said.

Shirlene pondered the Commission's offer and discussed the possibilities with her pastor who agreed it would be prudent to have the records microfilmed.

In the spring of 1989, Shirlene and Sep Love talked on the telephone and made final plans for him to pick up the records, which she was keeping in her home.

"I'll see you Monday week," Love had said as he hung up the telephone.

The week before Love was to come, the Gees left home early for church on Sunday night.

Before they had left home, Michael Gee had been listening to a television broadcast detailing the conditions favorable for a tornado.

"Weather's turning sour," Michael told his wife who was busy getting their preschooler, Seth, ready for church. Preoccupied, Shirlene gave little thought to the warnings.

"Could be headed our way," Michael said as he watched the skies turning the same yellow-green color that the weather forecaster had described.

Ignoring the weather, the Gees headed to church. Following the worship service, Shirlene was outside the church talking with friends when she saw a neighbor who had stopped in front of the church to talk with her brother-in-law.

Seeing their faces, Shirlene knew something was wrong.

"Someone has died," she thought to herself, wondering who had been struck by tragedy.

As her thoughts raced, Shirlene saw her brother-in-law approaching.

Tears rimmed his eyes, and Shirlene waited to

Lynn Grisard Fullman

hear the bad news.

"Your home is gone, destroyed by a tornado," he managed.

Shirlene dashed inside the church to find Michael and to tell him what had happened to the home they had built just two years earlier.

The couple raced to their car to speed home, pausing only to allow their pastor to insist on keeping their children, Seth and Jessica.

Shirlene and Michael raced home, spotting a few slightly damaged homes along the way and wondering just how badly Talladega had been hit.

Although all around things looked almost normal, that was not the case when the Gees saw what had been their home. The site where they had been just hours earlier looked more like a war zone than a homesite.

The roof had been lifted off and the walls had fallen, leaving a pile of rubble at their Eastaboga Road address.

The following morning, when Sep Love opened his newspaper, he saw on the front page a picture of Michael Gee picking through rubble that had been his home.

The newspaper account, like the picture, indicated that nothing had been saved.

Love, who was to see Mrs. Gee the next week, was heartsick.

"We came so close to saving the records and now they're gone. They're lost," he thought, folding the newspaper and feeling a lump in the pit of his stomach.

Knowing there would be no church records, Sep drove anyway to see Mrs. Gee, whom he had never met in person.

As Sep approached the spot where the Gees home had stood, he was heartsick all over again.

After introducing himself to Shirlene, he asked, "The records? Destroyed?"

Looking at the debris, he knew the answer almost before asking.

Shirlene smiled at the man she had just met.

"Last Sunday," she explained, "I don't know why, but I took the records to my father's house.

"They are safe."

Lynn Grisard Fullman

The answer comes

Bill Elder, Pastor
Over the Mountain Community Church
Birmingham, Alabama

Bill Elder had moved to Birmingham from Arkansas to become pastor of a Southern Baptist Church.

Before accepting the call, Bill had been told that the members were looking for new ways to reach others for Christ.

What Bill did not know, however, was which changes the congregation really wanted and which ones would be successful.

Lynn Grisard Fullman

One of his first innovations was the addition of a second Sunday morning worship service. Geared to young people, the service included more casual dress and the use of synthesizers, guitars and drums.

Like all changes, this one had a price. Members had to get used to new meeting times and new classes. More nursery workers were needed and the staff had to almost double their duties.

Although it was a bold step for the traditional congregation, most members embraced the changes.

Some members, however, did not like the new service and wanted it stopped.

Bill took their views seriously. He wanted all the members to support the new service, yet he could see that the service was touching lives, attracting new members and enlivening old members.

Yet, because of the discomfort for some, Bill considered discontinuing the second service. Maybe, for the sake of harmony, he thought, it would be best to go back to the old ways.

For days, he prayed, asking God for direction and guidance.

In his study one morning, Bill prayed and presented the facts to God. He asked for an answer, something to let him know one way or another if he should discontinue the second service.

Later that morning, with his prayer time over, Bill was in the church sanctuary where he was busy meeting with several members.

Although he had asked the church secretary not to interrupt his meeting, she came in anyway.

"Someone is here to see you," she announced.

Because she had not identified the visitor as a member of the church, he presumed someone had stopped by to ask for donations from the church's benevolence fund. It was not an unusual occurrence because of the church's visible location.

But he did not know why the secretary had interrupted him with the request.

Noticing a strange look on his secretary's face, Bill excused himself from the meeting.

Bill stepped into the nearby offices and saw a man who looked a bit puzzled. Nicely dressed, the man did not look like the usual person who would come asking for money.

"Can I help you?" Bill asked.

"I need to tell you something," the man started.

Bill asked the man into his office, closed the door and heard the story.

"I was driving by. I've done it a thousand times before, but his time, something told me to come in here.

"I have no idea what this means, but I had to come and tell you that 'the answer is no.' "

Although the visitor was confused, Bill knew that God had sent the answer that he had been seeking that morning.

Bill continued to support the second service.

Lynn Grisard Fullman

The voice

Vonnie Crimm
Sylacauga, Alabama

Rains were pounding the earth, winds were gusting and skies were dark. But, Vonnie Crimm had to get to work.

Despite the threatening weather, Vonnie, who was living in Gordo, got dressed and set out just before 4 a.m.

Struggling to see through the rains that pelted her car's windshield, she forged ahead.

When Vonnie was about a mile from home, rising water began to cover her tires. Undaunted, she continued.

"Oh, my cow," she thought as the waters splashed all around.

Lynn Grisard Fullman

She headed down a hill, her usual route to her job.

Then, out of nowhere, she heard a voice that demanded, "Turn around. Go back."

The voice was so compelling that Vonnie obeyed, turning the car around then heading back home. Maybe at dawn, she decided, she would try the drive again.

After she was home, her husband called to tell her he was glad she had not left for work.

The creek had risen, had flooded the bottom of the hill where she had been headed before the voice beseeched her to turn back.

The street had washed out, and the waters had carved a crater six feet deep and 10 feet wide.

The same rains, she later learned, had caused a similar washout in another location. And, at that site, a woman had died as her car had plunged into the hole caused by the flooding.

Vonnie did not know where the voice had come from, but she was glad she had listened. If she had not, she most likely would have died in the torrential rains.

It would be almost a decade before she would again hear the same voice.

Needing a large home to accommodate a growing family, she and her husband began searching Sylacauga for something they could afford and that would meet their needs.

The Crimms had searched the area high and low, but could not find the right house.

Then, one day as Vonnie was driving, she heard the voice again, the same voice that had told her to turn back on that stormy morning.

"Ride by and see if the house has sold," the voice demanded, mentioning a house that the Crimms had looked at several years earlier. Although they had fallen in love with the house then, they could not afford it.

Propelled by the voice, Vonnie drove by. To her surprise, the house that she remembered being so grand had become pathetic.

All 26 windows had been broken out, light fixtures had been removed, the swimming pool had been damaged, all the sheet rock pounded down.

When Vonnie told her husband Jimmy what she had seen, he made some calls. They learned that the couple who had lived in the once majestic house had divorced and the payments had not been made. Finding the house empty, vandals had ransacked it, leaving it in the disrepair that Vonnie had discovered.

The bank had foreclosed on the property, but was glad to entertain the Crimms offer which was thousands less than the asking price that had made the house previously unaffordable.

The Crimms renovated the house of their dreams.

And, they know that it was a house that was meant to be theirs—because the same voice that had lured Vonnie from harm's way a decade earlier had come back to direct her to

Lynn Grisard Fullman

the house.

"I think there's an angel watching over me," Vonnie says, adding, "and I'm glad it is."

If you need me, call me

Bernadette Wiggins
Birmingham, Alabama

Bernadette Wiggins had an ugly fight with her grandfather one night in the early 1980s.

Like most heated verbal battles, their disagreement led both of them to say things they shouldn't have.

"You'll be sorry," Bernadette admonished her grandfather, who was in his 70s.

"One day," she warned, "you'll get sick and I'll be the one who will have to take you to the hospital."

She wasn't certain why she reminded him

of his failing health, but at the time, the words just rolled out. They were, at the time, just another cruel thing to say.

In less than 24 hours, the old Alabama native did get sick.

And, because Bernadette lived with him, she was, as she had predicted, the one who drove him to the hospital.

Remembering their bitter words, the two drove in silence to St. Vincent's hospital on Birmingham's Southside.

Doctors there declared Andrew "Hot" Jackson sick enough to be admitted to the hospital. There appeared to be nothing life-threatening wrong with him, but he would need to stay, they told Bernadette.

Feeling lousy for the harsh things she had said to him hours earlier, Bernadette had a change of heart.

"Hot, if you need me, call me," she told her grandfather after he was settled in his hospital bed.

Then, as an afterthought, she added, "Even if you can't get to the phone, just call out my name. I'll hear you and I'll come."

With that, she was gone, driving home alone in the dark, thinking more about their bitter fight than Hot's health.

Once home, she crawled into bed, exhausted.

Just past midnight, something jerked her arm.

Too tired to care, she tried ignoring the shakes, but they continued.

When she dozed off, the tugging came

back.

When the yanking would not stop, she sat bolt upright in her bed.

"It's Hot," she thought to herself, "He's calling me."

Bernadette swung her bare feet onto the floor and reached for her clothes.

"I've got to get to the hospital. Hot needs me," she kept thinking as she struggled into her clothes.

Bernadette sped across town to the hospital. Without pausing to ask anyone if it were all right to visit at that late hour, she raced headlong to Hot's room.

He was asleep.

She sat beside him for a long time, but he never woke.

When a nurse came into the room, Bernadette, who was 21 then, told her about the jerks in her arm.

The nurse suggested there might be something wrong and had Bernadette taken to X-ray. But, as Bernadette had suspected, the film showed nothing wrong.

When Bernadette returned from X-ray to her grandfather's room, he rallied a bit. Opening his eyes, he smiled at her. "I'm glad you came," he said before drifting back to sleep.

Bernadette held Hot's hand a few more minutes. Then, as the wee hours of dawn seeped across the city, she slipped his hand from hers and left.

Lynn Grisard Fullman

The next morning, when Bernadette returned to the hospital, she saw first her mother and uncle.

They didn't need to say a word. Bernadette could read their faces. Hot was dead.

And, had she not been jolted from bed the night before, she would not have seen him that one last time.

Hot had called her, just as she had told him to—and she had heard.

The visitor

Janet Evans Turnure
Huntsville, Alabama

For the couple in Etowah County, it was a sad time. Their young daughter had been diagnosed with a terminal illness.

The child had been in and out of the hospital several times, each time seeming to lose ground from the weeks before.

"How can this be?" they asked each other, looking into the pale face of their child.

She should be romping and playing like other children her age, they thought. Instead, here she was, once again, lying on crisp white sheets in a hospital bed.

Nurses darted in and out of the room, bringing

Lynn Grisard Fullman

medicines and needles, smiles and pain.

It had been a weary experience for the family as they had watched their offspring suffer.

A good day would be followed by a day that they wanted only to push from their memories.

One evening, while the girl's father was out of the room, the mother sat beside her daughter's bed.

She stroked her hand and pushed her daughter's tousled hair out of her face, praying and feeling helpless.

It was at that moment a woman came into the room.

The visitor talked with the mother who unleashed her concerns.

"Don't worry," the visitor said softly, "she's going to be all right."

With that, the woman turned and left the room.

The mother, wondering who had visited, trailed her into the hallway and watched as she left.

No sooner had the visitor departed than the sick child's father returned.

"Someone was just here," his wife said as she began to tell about the visit.

"Who was it?" he asked.

"I have no idea," she admitted, "but she was so kind."

"As she was leaving," the mother recounted, "she touched my hand and assured me that everything will be all right. It gave me such peace."

Curious to find out who had taken the time to

visit, the husband glanced down the hallway where only minutes earlier the visitor had been.

"She went right through that door," the wife pointed, showing him where she last had seen the woman.

"Maybe I can catch her," the husband said, setting out in a slow trot, taking the same path the visitor had just taken.

When he got there, he pulled open the door where the visitor had exited.

It was a closet.

Lynn Grisard Fullman

Daddy's voice

Maudie Hammonds
Lineville, Alabama

On a summer day in 1980, Maudie Hammonds drove across a railroad track and was rounding a curve when she saw, looming in front of her, a white van.

Instinctively, she swerved to bypass the van whose owner, she assumed, had stopped alongside the rural road outside Clairmont.

It was a road she had traveled dozens of times, and it was a clear day.

Only this time, something went wrong. Terribly wrong.

For some reason, Maudie, who was 64 years old then, did not steer the car back into her lane.

Lynn Grisard Fullman

Instead, she never straightened out her curve, but drove, instead, off the road and plunged sixty feet.

Not wearing a seat belt, the Lineville resident was hurled from her car which kept tumbling until it came to rest upside down.

Addled after the plunge, Maudie lay in her own blood with pain searing her body.

Weary from her injuries and the pain, she did not know what to do.

She could hear cars passing by overhead and realized that no one could see her or her overturned car.

It was at that moment that Maudie's father, who had died the year before, appeared to her.

"Hey, Maud," her dad said, using the nickname that he alone had called her, "you got to get on the road. They can't see you down here."

"I can't," she whimpered, overtaken by fear and pain.

"Yes," he said in a soothing voice that was so familiar, "you can."

With her father's encouragement, Maudie, who had been lying in a puddle of blood, scratched and crawled part of the way up the bank.

Exhausted, she collapsed, unable to go any farther.

It was then that her father appeared a second time to her.

"There's not much farther to go," he calmly told her.

"You've got to keep going."

With that, Maudie started again, managing to reach the shoulder of the road where she collapsed, resting her bleeding head on her arms.

When next she heard the roar of an approaching car, Maudie wanted to raise her arms, wave them furiously and signal for help.

But, she wasn't able.

Instead of flailing her arms, she managed only to raise a single finger.

But, the finger was signal enough.

A car stopped, discovered an injured Maudie and got help for her.

Maudie recovered from her injuries.

And, to this day, she knows that it was her father who saved her by demanding that she do what she thought she could not do—crawl sixty feet uphill where she would find help.

Lynn Grisard Fullman

A path through flames

Macy Krupicka
Birmingham, Alabama

It was midnight when seven-year-old Macy Krupicka heard a loud noise.

During a stormy night when the Vestavia Hills resident was living in Oklahoma City, lightning struck her home's electrical circuits. Sparks flew from an outlet behind a couch. Within minutes, the couch was a mass of flames and the house was engulfed in smoke.

Macy could not see to get out. She called to her parents, but they could not hear her.

Lynn Grisard Fullman

The youngster walked to the foyer, but smoke and flames were everywhere, preventing her from reaching the front door.

Not knowing where to go, she stood in the foyer.

When she could not reach the front door, she thought of the back door. But, she knew all too well that her parents always kept that door locked with a deadbolt.

Afraid and standing in the foyer, little Macy was relieved when her father came.

When he folded his fingers around her tiny hand, she was filled with peace. She was, she knew, going to be safe, after all.

Her father led her to the back door. Even though the key to the deadbolt was never kept close to the door, she did not notice her father having any trouble getting the door open.

In the midst of the smoke and her own fears, she only noticed the door being opened and her father leading her to safety, outside in the rain.

He left her there, alone.

Even though she knew he probably went to help her mother or younger brother and sister, she did not want him to leave.

"Come back," she called. But, he was gone.

A few minutes later, Macy's mother found her in the back yard.

Relieved to see her daughter safe, Mrs. Krupicka asked how Macy had gotten out of the burning house.

"Daddy got me," the youngster answered.

About that time, her father found Macy and her mother and told them about narrowly making it through the flames as he carried Macy's brother and sister to safety.

The baby's eyelashes and eyebrows had been singed as he had struggled through the flames.

When those two were safe, Macy's father had tried to get back inside to find Macy. But, the flames had been too powerful.

He had never made it back inside for Macy.

Lynn Grisard Fullman

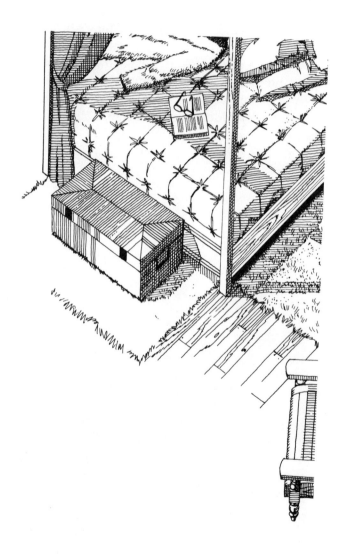

Memories in the wicker trunk

Gwen McCorquodale
Birmingham, Alabama

When Helen Jaye died, the whole town of Mexia mourned.

Florists around the south Alabama town sold out of flowers; and mourners could not be contained in the church where her funeral was held.

Memories of Mrs. Jaye's untimely death caused by an aneurysm were resurrected 18 months later when her home burned.

Mrs. Jaye's widower, David, was just beginning to pick up the pieces of his life when tragedy struck again.

David had left home one winter morning to visit one of his daughters who lived in Brewton, fifty miles away.

Before David reached Brewton, a relative had called to leave a message: "Your house is on fire."

Hearing the news, David jumped back into his car and headed home, wondering as he drove what he would find waiting.

Since his wife had died in the summer of 1983, David had not touched a thing in his house. Maybe, he thought now, he had been trying too hard to preserve her presence in the house where they had raised their four daughters.

Memories were both sweet and bitter as the girls and their father remembered earlier times when the six of them had been one.

The couple's daughters, not wanting to disrupt their childhood home, had refused to take any of their mother's things to their own homes.

Leaving things untouched had made the house still feel like home.

The fire, which started in a heat lamp in the shower, raged through the house.

On that freezing winter day, temperatures had plunged so low that the water sprayed onto the house froze before reaching its target. The firemen's efforts were in vain.

As the fire raged out of control, firemen on the scene could only hang their heads as they watched the house almost evaporate.

The flames were so hot that the ironing board and the silverware melted. All the things that the girls had hoped to one day have for their own were gone.

Even the large rocks on the fireplace facing crumbled into a heap.

As happens in rural towns, neighbors from near and far gathered to watch as the house burned.

"Can we help?" people asked.

"What can we do?"

The Jayes were grateful for the offers; but there was nothing anyone could do.

If they had one wish that day, they wanted family photos, reminders of their years together.

Even though the fire had begun at 8 a.m., throughout the day members of the volunteer fire department were summoned to battle simmering flames that would not be quenched.

As dusk settled over the tiny Alabama town south of Monroeville, David Jaye and his daughters took refuge in the home of relatives who lived nearby.

Memories, yes, were intact of the Christian lady who had been their family's matriarch; but the family wished for what they could not have. They wanted their family pictures, baby pictures, pictures of their parents as newlyweds, pictures of themselves as babies and children, graduating from high school and marrying as their parents looked on.

That night, as the family huddled together

and began considering how David could begin again, someone knocked on the front door.

David opened the door to find, in the cold, one of the volunteer firemen covered with soot and looking exhausted.

"You need to come with me," the fireman said.

"Now what?" the family thought as they slipped tired feet into their shoes and headed down the street to the simmering fire.

"Look at this," the fireman said, as he poked in the remains of the fire that had leveled the all-brick home, which dated to just after World War II.

In the rubble was a wicker chest which had stood beside a chair.

It was unharmed.

Inside the $40 chest were the family photos.

They were all that remained of the house where the Jayes had lived.

It was at that moment that the family knew that life would go on.

A bald-headed gimp and his guardian angel

Alan Pearce Holland
Thorsby, Alabama

As Alan Pearce Holland hung upside down from the running tractor, all he could think was, "I'm dead. I'm dead."

He had defied death a few years earlier when, at age 40, he had survived a debilitating stroke that had left his body partially paralyzed and his speech slurred.

Lynn Grisard Fullman

With patience and determination, the Thorsby resident had battled back after the stroke. He had learned to do things with his left hand and had found a way to operate the tractor, one of his farm chores that he always had enjoyed.

But, on this spring day in 1983, his luck seemed to have run out.

As Alan plowed the field, the tractor had run over a concrete block and jolted him from the seat. The only thing that spared Alan from sudden death or mutilation was his impaired right foot which somehow had wedged under the brake pedal.

"Mike, Mike," Alan screamed, hoping his young son would hear his cries.

But no help came. Above the roar of the tractor engine, Mike, inside the nearby house, could not hear his father's cries for help.

Alan dangled and bounced wildly from the out-of-control tractor, which tore across the field. As Alan swung from the tractor, the rear wheel spun and raced, ripping the skin from his back and leg.

"Nothing can save me now," Alan thought to himself as he flounced about and the tractor raced uncontrollably at full speed. He knew that if he fell, he would be mutilated by the raging tractor. Or, if his head flopped beneath the bush-hog blade, he would be maimed.

Above the roar of the tractor, he gave up calling for help and instead talked with God who had brought him through a host of other scrapes. Even though death loomed, Alan thanked God for his blessings and wondered what plans He could still have for, as he says, "a bald-headed gimp who I had thought was a defeated man."

Hanging upside down aboard the raging tractor, Alan watched as the machine aimed itself at a double row of barbed-wire fences.

"Not my will, but thine," he thought as he pinched his eyes closed, hoping not to linger too long after the tractor crashed through the fencing.

At the instant that Alan braced himself for the worst, the tractor's engine stopped.

Where moments earlier there had been the roar of an engine, now there was nothing but silence in that Alabama field. Alan could hear nothing but the thrashing of his heart.

With the tractor stilled, the muscles in Alan's hemiplegic leg relaxed, and he gently crumbled head-first onto the ground.

Too exhausted to call again for his son, Alan lay on the dirt as blood oozed from his injuries.

It took fifteen minutes for Alan's son to happen to leave the house and notice his dad lying beside the wayward tractor.

Mike called others to help, and within minutes, neighbors, Alan's parents and friends gathered to help.

One neighbor, known for his foul language, was among those who had a theory about why the tractor had finally stopped.

"The damn thing just ran out of gas," the cussing neighbor speculated.

Lynn Grisard Fullman

"But, the tank was full," Alan answered through clinched teeth as his mother wiped at his wounds.

"Probably the ignition wire pulled loose," another neighbor guessed.

"Maybe," Alan said, not certain that even he believed the theory.

"It was God looking after you," Alan's mother said quietly, as she bandaged his injuries that would take months to heal.

As several neighbors dashed outside to inspect the once-raging tractor, Alan couldn't help but agree with his mother.

For years he had believed that a guardian angel was on duty night and day protecting him.

As Alan thought of the angels who must stay busy keeping him from harm's way, he heard the tractor start on the first try.

A face
in the crowd

David Garst
Birmingham, Alabama
Gail Bullard
Trafford, Alabama

A lot of things had worked together to bring David Garst in 1984 to the waiting room of the State Employment Office.

David had graduated more than a decade earlier from Shelby County High School, had earned a degree in criminal justice from Auburn University, then moved to Atlanta.

But, the kid from Alabama still could not

Lynn Grisard Fullman

find himself.

He floundered at jobs, got tousled in relationships and knew he was not where he was meant to be. So, he pulled up stakes and headed home.

At age 30, David had a lot yet to prove not just to his parents who welcomed him back home, but to himself as he reentered college and struggled to find his life's work.

On this morning, David shifted on the chair and tried to get comfortable. He knew the wait would be long, and he knew the chances of finding a job were slim.

If he could find even a minimum-wage job, things would go more smoothly.

As David studied while he waited, he noticed a woman sitting several rows in front of him in the waiting room.

She would turn and look his way, then turn away. A few minutes later, she would steal another glance.

Trying to ignore her glimpses, David lost himself in his studies, as all around him people with solemn and frustrated-looking faces waiting their turns. David knew how they felt. He, too, was stymied in his job search. The economy was sluggish and jobs were scarce.

The woman, who had continued staring at David, finally left her seat and approached him.

"Need a job?" she asked, feeling rather silly for asking a question that had such an obvious answer. Why else would he be there?

David nodded.

"Can you type?" she asked, expecting that he probably couldn't.

"Yes," he answered as he wondered where the conversation might be headed.

In the back of Gail Bullard's mind, she was thinking of a job one of her customers had available. The candidate needed to be a college student willing to work evenings.

Gail doubted that David fit the criteria for the job available at Burlington.

"Could you work nights?" she asked, still embarrassed that she was asking and still trying not to notice her heart pounding wildly in her chest.

"I not only can, I have to," David answered, explaining that as a full-time student, he was involved in school weekdays 8 a.m. to 5 p.m.

"But, can you enter information into a computer?" she asked, assuming she had finally asked the question that would end the conversation.

David nodded that he could.

Gail, an outside salesperson, handed the young man her business card, and on the back she wrote the name of the company looking for a new employee.

"Tell them I sent you," she said.

That morning, Gail had gone to the employment office with her sister-in-law. And, within minutes of Gail's conversation with David, her sister-in-law was back from her interview and ready to leave. Heading out the door, Gail wished David good luck.

The next time Gail called on Burlington, she asked about the student she had sent to apply for the job.

Burlington knew nothing about him. Gail went away feeling justified that she had been right in wanting to quell that nagging prompting that had led her to tell the young man about the job.

Several weeks later, when Gail returned again to the business, she asked a second time.

"I don't suppose that fellow ever came about the job," she asked, hardly waiting for their reply.

"Sure did," they said, "and he's wonderful."

From time to time, as Gail returned to the business, she asked about the college student she had met in the State Employment Office.

Every time, the company had nothing but good things to say about the man who seemed he had been made for the job.

David kept the job until he graduated from occupational therapy school in December 1986. In the spring of 1987, he landed a job at St. Vincent's Hospital where he still works as a staff occupational therapist. It is a job he never intends to leave, because, as he says, "I'm where I'm supposed to be."

The job at Burlington had financed David's education.

The job brought together a culmination of David's life - the chance to use his counseling talents, to bring empathy to those who, like he, had had rough times in their lives, to capitalize on his criminal justice degree that once had seemed useless.

The day that Gail Bullard met David Garst, she had prayed to be God's instrument.

And, as she had waited for her sister-in-law to job hunt, she somehow had singled out one man among the crowd.

She had not wanted to approach the bearded young man.

But that day, a demanding voice would give her no peace.

"He's the one. Tell him," the voice had prodded.

Lynn Grisard Fullman

A voice in the dark

Kennith Bishop
McCoy Memorial United Methodist Church
Anniston, Alabama

In the 1950s, Kennith Bishop was just out of the Army and still deciding what to do with his life.

Waiting to choose his life's path, he took a job in Chicago with Superior Marking Products, a company that made ink, type trays, date stamps and toy printing presses.

Bishop's job was to operate a vacuum press, hardly the work that seemed it would, in time, lead him to become a Methodist minister in Ala-

Lynn Grisard Fullman

bama.

At Superior, Bishop got to know his co-workers. Joe, a burly man with a deep faith, was one of Bishop's favorites.

Joe had worked three decades with the company and his seniority and wisdom brought respect from other workers.

Whenever Joe would talk, others would listen, clinging to his words and his memories dating to his early years with the company.

Bishop never listened more intently than he did one afternoon when Joe, during a coffee break, told about something that had happened to him years earlier. And, it had happened in the plant.

Joe remembered an evening when he had gone into a warehouse which was something he had done dozens of times before.

Even though the warehouse was dark, Joe had no qualms about entering the gloom where he knew his way around.

His footsteps echoed as he stepped across the floor. When Joe finished his work in the warehouse, he headed for the freight elevator.

Just as he was about to step into the elevator, Joe heard someone calling his name.

"Joe. Joe." the voice said.

Joe turned to look around, but saw no one.

"Who's there?" he called back. But, there was no answer.

Joe presumed one of the guys was playing a trick on him. A second time, he asked who was in the darkness. Again, there was no answer.

Shrugging his shoulders, Joe turned and headed toward the elevator.

But, because his eyes had had time to grow accustomed to the darkness, this time he could see what waited ahead—an elevator shaft.

The elevator car, where moments earlier he had almost stepped, had never arrived.

Had Joe not turned to the voice in the darkness, he would have plunged into the shaft and to his death.

Lynn Grisard Fullman

Baby in bricks

Johnnie Woods
Oakman, Alabama

Newlywed in the early 1900s, Gertrude and Rich set out for a walk one Sunday afternoon.

It was long before the days of televisions and cars, and Sunday strolls were common entertainment.

The couple walked a couple of miles from their north Alabama house when they came upon an abandoned homestead.

Remains of a brick fireplace had tumbled among the fruit trees.

As Rich and Gertrude prowled over the land, they heard what sounded like a baby crying.

As they moved closer, they were certain that

Lynn Grisard Fullman

the sound was coming from beneath the crumbled bricks.

"What could it be?" she asked him, not waiting to see him shrug his shoulders.

The two bolted for the brick heap and began looking.

They shoved hunks of bricks from side to side above the spot where they thought they heard the sounds.

When they would reach the ground, the sound would move, seeming to come from another spot.

"Over here," Rich pointed, as he moved to another place and began tossing bricks aside.

Gertrude joined him, flinging bricks and wondering what could be trapped there.

"Sounds like a baby," she said, and Rich nodded in agreement.

The sun began to set and the couple realized they had to head back down the road to their home where evening chores waited.

It was the hardest thing the two ever had to do, but they left as the baby's cries pierced the night.

As the couple approached their house, Rich's brother ran to meet them.

With one look at his face, they knew that something terrible had happened.

"It's Mary," he said, referring to his wife.

"She died, just a little while ago, giving birth to our daughter."

"Will you take her?" he asked.

The couple, who only minutes earlier had been

haunted by the wails of a baby in need, looked into each other's eyes.

They looked back at Rich's brother.

"Yes," they said.

Lynn Grisard Fullman

A final piece of business

Hazel Metzler
Birmingham, Alabama

Sister Mary Jude Clark
Cullman, Alabama

It was strange, actually, how Hazel Metzler got to know Sister Clare, who for more than fifty years taught at St. Paul's Catholic Church School.

Their relationship started when Hazel made good on a promise she had made with God. Praying for her husband to survive the life-threatening

Lynn Grisard Fullman

injuries sustained in a car accident, Hazel had vowed she would work for God if her husband would live.

Bob lived, and Hazel, after his recovery, began working as a teacher's aide at St. Paul's in downtown Birmingham.

It was there that Hazel, with only an eighth grade education, got to know Sister Clare.

The two were close.

Hazel remembers Sister Clare calling on her for all kinds of help.

"Mrs. Metzler," the teacher would say, "would you do me a favor?"

And, for the eight years that Hazel knew Sister Clare, she did help.

Anytime the sister couldn't be in the classroom, Hazel, following specific instructions left by Sister Clare, would teach the kindergarten and first grade students.

Sometimes, Sister Clare would ask Hazel to run errands or drive her to appointments.

There was a special bond between the two women, one who had married the church and one who was the mother of five children.

Sister Clare was generous with Hazel, giving her small gifts like a rosary or books relating to the Catholic religion that Hazel had converted to after her marriage to Bob.

One time, Sister Clare gave Hazel a piece of cloth that had been part of a saint's robe. Another time, she gave her some holy water from Lourdes.

In 1980, Sister Clare, who had been like a mother to Hazel, got sick.

Hazel was in the school office one day when the school principal, Sister Mary Jude Clark, received a phone call from the hospital.

Somehow, Hazel knew. Sister Clare was dead.

Hazel missed Sister Clare, who was 83 when she died.

Hazel missed teaching with her, missed their long conversations, missed the woman who had encouraged her, who had stood by her when her husband had almost died.

Sister Clare, the woman who had given her life to her church, was buried on a Tuesday with a full send off, complete with several priests and a requiem mass.

As the sister's casket, draped with a cross, was rolled down the aisle of St. Paul's, the pall bearers paused, as fate would have it, beside the aisle where Hazel sat.

It was the last time that the two women would be physically close together.

Tears streamed down Hazel's face as she watched the slow procession.

Two weeks after Sister Clare had been laid to rest in Sacred Heart Monastery in Cullman, Hazel had had a hectic morning.

After getting her youngest two children off to school on a rainy day, Hazel slipped back into bed for a quick nap.

As she slept, something strange happened.

Lynn Grisard Fullman

In her sleep, Hazel saw and spoke with Sister Clare who was walking up a long and slanting hallway that had no doors.

Sister Clare had a load of white clothes draped across her arm.

"I wonder why she's going to do the laundry?" Hazel thought as she looked at the nun who was wearing her customary black habit, the same one that she had been buried in.

Passing by Hazel, Sister Clare smiled, showing the gold cap on her front tooth.

Just as Sister Clare had passed, she looked back across her shoulder and said those words that Hazel had heard a hundred times before.

"Mrs. Metzler," she asked, "would you do me a favor?"

Hazel nodded that she would.

"Would you go tell Sister Mary Jude that there's something important in my things she needs to tend to."

Then, Sister Clare turned her back and kept walking up the long hallway where two other nuns, dressed in white, waited for her.

One of the nuns was Sister Mary Thomas who had taught Hazel's son in first grade. She, like Sister Clare, was dead.

With that, Hazel was awake, returned to reality, the rainy day in Birmingham and the dirty dishes in the sink.

For several days she thought about the dream and she almost told Sister Mary Jude the message.

"She'll think I'm nuts," Hazel decided, shoving aside the compelling urge to pass the message along.

The third morning after the dream, Hazel had to tell.

She called Sister Mary Jude, who was in the convent where the nuns lived next door to the downtown school.

"I know you left instructions not to be disturbed," she apologized as Sister Mary Jude listened on the other end.

"I have to give you a message."

Hazel told the sister about the dream that had seemed so real. After hearing, Sister Mary Jude explained that she had just finished cleaning out Sister Clare's drawers and shelves.

She had found nothing out of the ordinary, no unfinished business.

In fact, to be certain she had not missed a thing, she had gone through the drawers and shelves a second time after emptying them.

She was convinced—nothing more was there.

No, Sister Mary Jude comforted Hazel, she did not think Hazel was crazy, but neither did she have an explanation for what had happened.

The more Sister Mary Jude, who was principal at St. Paul's 32 years, thought about the haunting message, she decided to take one last look.

Using a fingernail file, Sister Mary Jude pried

up the linoleum that lined the shelves where Sister Clare had kept her things.

It was under that lining—on the shelf that Mary Jude had declared empty—that she found something.

On the shelf, under the linoleum, were cash and checks totaling almost $500. It was money that Sister Clare had collected from her students for their first communion supplies—prayer books, veils and rosaries.

Sister Mary Jude, at Sister Clare's request, had handled the final piece of business.

Home for the holiday

Sam Aaron
Nauvoo, Alabama

If anyone had any doubts about the young couple's future together, they had only to wait. Lorene and Buel Aaron were meant to be, especially by today's standard when so many young folks end their marriages in divorce.

Lorene was only sixteen when she married Buel in 1936.

As the country struggled to put the economic depression behind, the Jasper couple had their eye and hearts on tomorrow, not yesterday.

Lynn Grisard Fullman

Six years her senior, Buel had a way of looking out for his bride, and people couldn't help but notice.

Buel loved his family and holidays spent with them. He especially loved Christmas when stockings were hung, the tree was decorated with twinkling lights and the smell of cooking turkey filled the kitchen.

Even after their children were grown and had families of their own, Buel and Lorene cherished the times they could be together.

In 1986, the couple, surrounded by children and grandchildren, celebrated their fifth decade together.

Not every day had been a honeymoon. Anybody who says they never fought, Lorene says today, can't be telling the truth.

Marriages, like everything else in life, have good and bad times.

What counts, bottom line, is that the two stick together, resolve their differences and make their union work, she says.

Life together was good for the Aarons, even though Buel suffered with black lung, a miner's affliction caused by years of breathing coal dust.

The joy of their decades together came to a close when Buel was 74. Two years after their golden wedding anniversary, in the summer of 1988, Buel died in a Jasper hospital.

Two Christmases later, Lorene had just returned home from a Birmingham hospital. She had

had serious surgery on her spine, and the family was pleased she had recovered enough to be home for the holidays.

As most families do when they gather, they took pictures, which would last for years as a reminder of the time spent together.

That Christmas, the Aarons' son, Sam, was the photographer.

"Okay," he said, "ya'll stand over here," he said, pointing to the television set in his mother's home.

There was too much commotion for the television to be on that day, but it became the backdrop for the photos capturing the Christmas spent in Lorene's new trailer. She had moved there not long after her husband's death.

Buel had not lived there with her, but he had helped to make the decision to buy it and had signed the papers not long before death had snatched him away.

Kids were talking and giggling and nobody really seemed to be cooperating as Sam tried to gather everyone for pictures.

"Smile," he said, as he clicked the camera.

"One more time," he added and snapped another picture.

He took several pictures that day with various family members standing together and making their best smiles.

Christmas soon melted into New Year's and another year rolled into place.

Everyone had forgotten the film, still in the camera with a final shot or two needing to be taken.

In July, Sam finally got around to taking the Christmas pictures to be developed.

When he brought the pictures home and began looking at them, he saw something that convinced him that Christmases really are for being together.

On the television screen and wearing his best suit, the same one he had been buried in, was a familiar face.

It was Buel.

He had come to spend Christmas with his family.

Lost overalls; spared life

S.W. "Woody" Castleberry
Birmingham, Alabama

Money was scarce in the 1930s, not just in Alabama, but across the nation which still was crawling out of an economic depression never before or since rivaled.

A kid in those days was lucky just to have clothes, whether handed down by a neighbor or an older sibling. To get something new was unheard of.

But, Woody Castleberry, who today is retired and living in Vestavia Hills, got a brand-new pair of

Lynn Grisard Fullman

overalls in the 1930s.

The youngster couldn't believe his luck. The pants actually fit and they were 401s, the kind that everybody wished they had.

Sporting his new clothes, Woody left his Walker County home one evening to spend the night with his friend, who lived a couple of football fields' distance up the road.

The sounds of crickets filled the warm night air as Woody skipped to his friend's house.

School was out and the world was just right for the seven year old—especially one who had new overalls.

Woody and his friend played outside well past dark. Then, they went inside.

Before tumbling into bed, both boys hung their overalls on the bedposts.

But, Woody's friend did not have the same new 401s that Woody had. His, like the ones Woody had just handed down to his little brother, were faded and getting too short and too tight.

After whispering a while, the boys fell asleep only to be wakened by crashing sounds in the next room.

Woody's friend explained that his brother had come home drunk and it promised to be an ugly scene, as it always was when he drank too much.

"You'd better go home before it gets worse," Woody's buddy urged.

In the dark, Woody reached for his overalls and bolted out the door, hoping not to be caught in the crossfire of whatever the drunk brother was hurling around the house.

Racing up the dirt road, Woody struggled to run and pull on his overalls at the same time.

"Funny," he thought, "they feel too little."

It was then that the youngster realized that he had grabbed his friend's britches. His still were hanging in the dark on the bedpost.

"Tomorrow," he thought, "I'll go back. No way I'm going tonight."

When Woody reached home, his family was asleep. Because back then nobody locked their doors, Woody tiptoed in and crawled into his own bed as his heart still pounded, partly out of fear of the enraged brother and partly because he had almost set speed records sprinting home.

Woody woke the next morning to the sounds of his mother weeping in the next room.

He walked up behind her to see her staring into the distance where smoke spiraled into the clear morning.

About that time, Woody saw his daddy trudging up the road, his head lowered, his voice soft.

"It's too late," his dad called to his mother.

"There's nothing left, just a few burning embers, everything is destroyed."

Woody's mother waled as she looked toward the neighboring house.

Woody suddenly realized what had happened. The house where he had left his overalls had burned to the ground.

"Mama," he called, stepping around where she could see him.

The young woman, tears streaming down her face, stooped to embrace the child she had believed was dead.

An instinct saves a family

Julianne Phillips
Birmingham, Alabama

The newlywed couple had been out for dinner one evening in 1957. They rode home that night silently, content with their meal and their lives.

Julianne Phillips had told her husband Bill about a sense of direction that had guided her life. This night, she would tell him again.

"Birds know where to find food to eat to stay alive, so why wouldn't people have an extra sense directing them?"

"Sometimes," she had said, "I hear an inner

Lynn Grisard Fullman

voice that gives me direction. I feel that God tells me where to go."

That night, the voice spoke vividly to her.

"Honey," she blurted, "we've got to pull off the road now."

Although they had been married only a year, it had been long enough for Bill to realize that the directings she sensed were compelling.

"Okay," he muttered, wishing they could keep going so he could get home and get some sleep.

Bill pulled the car to the side of the road and turned off the engine.

Julianne sat quietly, waiting to better understand what she must do.

Only the sounds of crickets and a distant barking dog filled the night air in central Alabama.

"There's someone's house where we have to go," she told Bill.

"Okay," he responded in defeat as he shrugged his shoulders and revved the car's engine.

"Where?" he asked, waiting directions.

She explained that they needed to go to the house of one of her high school friends who was married and had a young family.

"But, it's midnight," Bill protested.

"Doesn't matter," she answered quickly. "We've got to go. And, we've got to go now."

"I'm not disturbing these people at this hour," he balked, but his wife was not to be discouraged.

"Well, just drive me there and I'll go in," she

countered.

Because the couple were not far from the house where Julianne believed they needed to go, it took only a few minutes for them to reach the house.

There were no lights shining inside the house, and outside there were no cars. From outward appearances, it seemed that no one was home.

"You go around back and I'll go to the front," Julianne instructed as she dashed from the car.

Sensing the mounting urgency, she explained to Bill, "We've got to get in."

Julianne pounded on the wooden front door, then paused to listen for footsteps inside. She heard nothing. Out back, her husband also was knocking, but he, too, saw and heard no one inside.

Again, she beat on the door.

At last, a tiny woman, the wife of Julianne's friend, cracked the door to see what had caused so much commotion.

"Please, can I come in?" she implored.

"Okay," the woman said in a voice as tiny as her frame.

Even in the dark, Julianne could see that the woman was wearing baby-doll pajamas.

When she stepped inside, Julianne saw for the first time that the woman was clutching a gun.

"I must have frightened you and I'm sorry," she began, reaching to take the gun from the woman's trembling hand.

Struggling to see in the dark house where only

Lynn Grisard Fullman

a nightlight burned, Julianne sat the gun on top of the television set.

"I was in the bedroom where the boys are sleeping," the young woman explained.

Glancing around the house, Julianne saw no signs of her high school friend. He must have, she thought, taken the car, leaving his wife and children home alone.

When Julianne turned on a lamp, she saw that the woman had been beaten. Her eye was swollen and tears streaked her bruised face.

"We'd been to a party and he'd been drinking," the woman began, as she plunged into an explanation. The beating, she said, was not the first.

"When we got home," she continued, "he finally got so mad that he left. I had taken it for as long as I could. That's when I got the gun out."

For the first time, Julianne realized that the woman had not reached for the gun because she heard the pounding and feared an intruder.

"Just before you came, I had asked the Lord to forgive me," she sobbed.

"I was going to kill the boys and then myself."

The day it didn't rain

Kennith Bishop
Anniston, Alabama

The congregation at the small Adamsville church had been saving for months to build an education building.

Members of the Methodist church had long ago outgrown their meeting spaces and had been holding Sunday morning classes in the choir loft and in corners of the sanctuary.

Badly in need of more space, the membership worked to raise enough money for an education building. But once the money was together, constant rains continued to delay the project.

The morning when the concrete floor was scheduled to be poured, Pastor Kennith Bishop was up early. At 5 a.m., he saw the sky filled with dark clouds.

"Not today," he thought, disappointed to see the project delayed yet another day. He called to tell the contractor that the project would have to be postponed until a better day.

Bishop knew that once he ordered the concrete to be poured, he was committed. If it rained on the concrete before it had had time to dry, it would be ruined.

An hour later, when the dark clouds had passed and it looked as though the weather was improving, Bishop made a difficult decision—he called the contractor again. This time, he gave the go-ahead.

Once ordered, the concrete would have to be paid for. If the cost of the concrete and the crew was wasted, the tiny church's dream of a new building might never come true. Or, at best, it would be delayed until members could raise more money.

An hour and a half after ordering the concrete to be sent, the minister went to the church to wait for the workers. But, by then, the sky had turned dark and rains threatened.

Bishop's heart was heavy and his eyes filled with tears as he looked first at the building site and back to the road to watch for the concrete trucks and the workers.

As clouds swirled overhead, Bishop walked to the center of what would become an education building. With tears filling his eyes, he knelt to pray.

"Don't let it rain today, Lord," he asked.

Then, thinking that perhaps somewhere someone needed the rain, he changed his prayer.

"Lord," he asked, "just don't let it rain right here."

Within a few minutes, the crews arrived. Readying the earth for the concrete to be poured went smoothly as clouds swirled overhead.

At noon, with the skies clear and several hours of work left to do, the workers left for lunch.

Almost in a panic, the crew returned within a few minutes to report that all around them, rains were pounding so hard they had not been able to get out of their trucks.

The men worked tirelessly, running to finish before the downpour inched closer.

Dark clouds hovered, the smell of rain filled the air, a few drops of rain fell.

To the east and to the west, rains pelted the earth.

But, on the site where concrete was smoothed and waiting to cure, the rains that day never fell.

Lynn Grisard Fullman

Beating the odds to regain a life

Sarah Little
Birmingham, Alabama

It was a morning that seemed like any other for the Little family. Les and Sarah were headed to work and their daughters were off to school.

A surgical nurse, Sarah had not been gone long when a car forced her off the highway south of Birmingham.

Spinning out of control, Sarah's car was

Lynn Grisard Fullman

broadsided, ejecting her from the driver's seat, hurling her like a ragdoll 30 feet through the air.

Sarah landed on her head.

Unconscious, the 40-year-old mother of two was rushed to the hospital.

As she lay in a coma, she glided into a beautiful place where she saw Jesus wearing a long robe.

He was very busy and standing with His back to her.

"Sarah," he told her, "I want you to go back to your husband and two girls. They need you."

Sarah obeyed, returning to her family, but her fight was far from over.

For more than 16 weeks in 1964, she laid unconscious in the hospital while doctors expected her to die.

But, Sarah clung onto a thread of the life she had been told to return to.

When time brought no progress, doctors suggested that her husband take her home where a familiar environment might ease her transition back into reality.

Three months after the accident, Les took Sarah home, but nothing seemed familiar to her.

A month later—four months after the accident—Sarah began to rouse, like a baby waking from a long night's sleep. Little by little, the world began to register.

At one point, she confided to her daughter that she might want to marry "that man" who was taking care of her. The man was Les, her husband, the father of her daughters.

Even though Sarah had no scars, the wreck had taken its toll, leaving her brain damaged. She had trouble talking and walking and much of her memory had been erased.

Therapists tried in vain to teach her to walk, but gave up when they determined that she did not have enough balance. She would, they said, never walk again.

For more than twenty years, Sarah sat in a wheelchair, trapped in a damaged body. Although she could not walk, she could think clearly.

It was in that chair that Sarah learned a patience that she never before had known.

She longed during those days and years to leave the confines of the chair.

She wanted so much to be active again, to play with her children, to walk in a shopping center.

One day, a thought came to her: try it again, try to walk, try to get out of this chair.

Confiding the fantasy to Les, Sarah returned for therapy more determined than ever, more convinced than ever that she would walk.

Hour after hour she moved listless limbs, driven by a desire to one day stand and walk down the aisle of her church. That place, she thought, would be the perfect place to show what prayer and persistence and belief could accomplish.

As Sarah returned to therapy, some days went better than others.

Some days, she thought she might just as well

slump back into the wheelchair and abandon her dream.

She clung to the hope that her brain had healed more thoroughly—and she clung to a promise in the Bible: "Don't be afraid. Just stand where you are and watch, and you will see the wonderful way the Lord will rescue you today." (Exodus 14:13).

Other times, though, Sarah knew she had to keep on, she owed that much to her friends who had, with her, prayed and believed in a miracle.

One day, in her regular prayer for her miracle, Sarah seemed to hear the voice of Jesus saying, "It is time to try again."

Sarah Little's miracle came in 1987.

Three months after beginning therapy, which she had kept secret from everyone but Les, Sarah did what she had promised herself to do as a testimonial to God's faithfulness and the power of prayer.

On a Sunday morning in late summer, Sarah left her wheelchair behind and, using a pronged cane, walked the aisle of her church.

There was not a dry eye as Sarah Little claimed her miracle and grasped the answer to a 23-year-old prayer.

A mother knows

Doug Swain
Oxford, Alabama

Stationed with the Air Force in Biloxi, Mississippi in the early 1970s, Airman First Class Doug Swain used to, on the spur of the moment, leave after work on Fridays and drive home to Tuscaloosa.

His parents never knew when to expect their son, who worked in the hospital lab. But they always were glad whenever they would wake to hear Doug's jeep rumbling into the driveway in the morning's wee hours.

One weekend in the fall of 1973, Doug decided

Lynn Grisard Fullman

to head home.

As he laced his way north through Mississippi just past Meridian, something happened that almost ended his young life.

On a two-lane road in the dark of night, a truck sped headlong in Doug's lane as he drove over a bridge.

When Doug saw the truck racing his way, he looked for a way out.

In an instant, Doug weighed his options. The opposite lane was empty, but the truck might swerve back where it belonged. To Doug's right, there were no guard rails, only pilings that might have broken his plunge down a sharp riverbank.

As Doug tried to slow his car, the headlights raced toward him, as though not to see him.

Doug watched the lights speeding closer toward his jeep.

"There's no place to go," he thought, as panic began to set in. "What can I do?"

Still, the lights sped his way.

Doug blinked his lights, from high to low then back again, hoping to catch the attention of the driver who was zooming toward him. It wasn't much of an effort, but it was all Doug could do.

Then, just inches from the front of Doug's jeep, the lights jerked to the left, and the driver continued down the highway.

When the lights zipped past, it was then that Doug could see that it had been a pickup truck that almost had crashed head-first into him.

Shaken by the thoughts of death having whisked so near, Doug drove the rest of the way home.

He expected to arrive to a dark house and sleeping parents the way he always had.

Instead, he found the lights on and his mother sitting up.

Relieved to be at home and safe, Doug considered not telling his mother about his close call. "No need to worry her," he thought.

But, he couldn't resist telling.

"I was almost killed tonight," Doug said, trying to sound calm as he remembered the truck racing straight toward him.

"I know," his mother answered in a calm voice. Then, she told Doug the very minute that the accident almost had occurred.

"But, Mom," Doug interrupted, "you didn't even know I was coming home."

"I just had this feeling," she explained. "Something said, `Pray for Doug's safety on the highway' --and I prayed.

"Then, I waited for you to come."

Lynn Grisard Fullman

The curve

Lois Fulford
Tuscaloosa, Alabama

On a fall night as dark as ink, Lois Fulford struggled to keep her Volkswagen Beetle on the Tuscaloosa road near Forest Lake.

She and her teenage daughter, Era, were chatting, making small talk to pass the time as they rode through the darkness.

Light pouring from nearby houses lit their path. But, once the duo had passed the homes, darkness again shrouded their way.

Just beyond the houses, the unlit street took a very sharp turn.

As Lois drove toward the curve, her Volkswagen's steering wheel refused to be turned.

Lynn Grisard Fullman

It felt as though someone were wrestling with her, trying to turn right as she struggled to turn left. Lois would gain an inch, then lose an inch as she fought to direct the car into the turn.

When it became obvious that she could not steer the car into the curve, Lois began looking for the most harmless path to take.

"Maybe no harm would be done if we go over there," she thought, as the car headed straight into someone's backyard.

It happened so quickly, Lois did not have time to think what could be wrong with her car. She had never had the problem before, and, as far as she knew, there was nothing wrong with the car's steering column.

She slammed on the brake and gripped the steering wheel, guiding the car off the pavement and bringing it slowly to a halt. As the car seemingly directed itself off the pavement, Lois brought it quickly to a stop.

Lois and Era sat quietly for a minute as they tried to piece together what had happened, what had prevented the car from turning into the curve.

"I just don't know," Lois told her daughter on that night in 1969. "I kept trying to turn, but I just couldn't."

As mother and daughter talked, a man suddenly appeared at the car window. She had not seen the man before that moment.

"You all right in there?" he asked as he leaned into the car.

"Uh, yeah," they finally muttered, not sure where the man had come from.

Afraid of the man who wreaked of alcohol, Lois drove away, leaving him standing alone.

This time, without resisting, the car turned into the curve.

It was the same curve where minutes earlier the man had been standing.

Had Lois been able to turn the steering wheel, she would have crashed headlong into the man.

Lynn Grisard Fullman

The well

Ann Cantrell
Sulligent, Alabama

Ann Cantrell, a newlywed in the early 1950s, lived in Sulligent where she and her groom rented a farmhouse.

The house sat at the end of a winding rural road where workers earlier had dug all kinds of holes in search of water.

Water eventually had been found close to the house and the useless holes had remained uncapped. By today's regulations, it would be considered a hazard, but in those days, the oversight was routine.

One day, Ann carried some unhatched chicken eggs to one of the shallow holes that she had been

Lynn Grisard Fullman

using for her garbage dump.

The hole was away from the house at the edge of the woods.

When she tossed the eggs into the cavity, they cracked open, revealing tiny chickens.

"Maybe they'll live," she thought, as she jumped in to get the eggs.

No sooner had she plunged than she had to laugh at herself.

"What in the world am I doing in here?" she mused as she stood ankle-deep in the rubble.

A few things crunched and cracked as she stepped to reach the eggs.

With the agility of her nineteen years, she hopped out of the hole, realizing that the rescued chickens had no chance of surviving.

She kicked the chunks of garbage from her feet and headed back to the house, giving little thought to her rescue attempt.

As she usually did in the early morning, Ann the next day trudged up the hill to toss garbage into the void that had not produced water.

Looking at the would-be well, she realized that someone years earlier, in trying to fill the cavern, had crammed in limbs and other debris.

That was why the hole had seemed more shallow than the others that had been abandoned.

But, this morning, the hole was different.

It had caved in.

The bottom, where she had stood, had tumbled one-hundred feet into the bowels of the earth.

Beating the odds for two

Carolyn Withrow
Birmingham, Alabama

Lora Ort slumped sleepily against the back window of the car as her year-old daughter, sitting in her carseat, nuzzled against her.

It was just after Christmas, 1991, and little Katherine already was excited about the toy radio that Santa three days earlier had left beneath her Christmas tree.

Lynn Grisard Fullman

Lora woke and decided to move into the car's front seat where her husband Michael, a medical intern, was navigating their car through the streets of Montgomery.

Getting settled, Lora adjusted the seat belt, making sure not to put too much pressure across her abdomen where already her three months of pregnancy were beginning to show.

Within minutes of buckling herself and Katherine into place, Lora's world went into a tailspin.

A car slammed into Lora's side of the car, mutilating the very section where only minutes earlier she had slept.

Glass shattered and steel twisted as the car spun out of control like a remote-controlled car being operated by an unseen force.

Lora was thrown with such force against the seat belt that her collar bone broke. Katherine and her dad were tossed around like sock dolls. But, it was Lora who caught the brunt of the crash.

Within minutes, paramedics, who by chance were nearby, arrived at the accident and began emergency measures to save Lora's life.

Once she was transported to the hospital emergency room, doctors evaluated Lora's injuries.

They shook their heads as they broke the news to Lora's husband.

"At best," they said, "we can only give her a 20 percent chance of surviving. I wish we could tell you more, but it doesn't look good."

With his medical training, Michael knew all too well what they meant when they talked of punctured lungs, head injuries, a ruptured spleen, a half dozen broken ribs and a broken collar bone.

"She's pregnant," Michael told the doctors who were treating his wife.

Michael knew that Lora's health, at this point, took priority over the unborn baby's, but he couldn't help but worry about the baby, too.

Michael next had to phone Lora's parents, Carolyn and Larry Withrow, who lived in Birmingham where Lora had grown up.

"Mom," he said, "there's been an accident."

As Carolyn listened, everything went fuzzy. She looked around her home and the glitter faded from the Christmas decorations that she had not yet put away. The Withrows jumped into their car and sped to Montgomery to be with their daughter and to help with baby Katherine who, like her father, had received minor bumps and bruises in the accident.

After the Withrows arrived and Lora was stabilized, doctors took Lora into surgery where they raced the clock to stop internal bleeding.

"It doesn't look good," the doctors reminded Lora's family, who refused to give up hope for her survival.

"There's no way to know how long oxygen was cut off from her brain," the doctors reminded her family, bracing them for the enormous disabilities that their wife and daughter could face should she

Lynn Grisard Fullman

live. No one dared to imagine what might become of the baby she carried.

Hearing the news that seemed to grow gloomier from day to day, Lora's family could only shake their heads. Yes, they heard the doctors. But, no, they would not give up on this spry young woman who had been a high school track star.

The reality set in as Lora's family considered the odds. If one hundred people had suffered the same injuries, only 20 would live. If 10 had, only two would survive.

Although the news was not good, Lora's family could only pray and wait, taking turns being at her side, listening for word from her doctors, hoping they would see signs that she was responding.

When her massive head injuries caused seizures, doctors gave Lora medicines to prevent them. Even though the medicines should not have been given to an expectant mother, the doctors had no choice. They had to weigh the risk against the cost of Lora's survival.

As Lora lingered, the doctors continued high-calorie nourishment, hoping against hope to sustain the tiny life that grew within her.

Six weeks after the accident, Lora began to respond. She opened her eyes and stared at the waiting and haggard faces of her family.

"She may not know you," doctors had warned, and Lora's family braced for that possibility.

Lora looked at her husband, then at her mother. She stared blankly into their faces, and then she smiled.

She knew Michael. She knew her mother. She knew her father.

It was at that moment Michael slipped Lora's wedding ring back onto her finger.

When Lora grew more stable, she was moved to a rehabilitation hospital where she learned again all the basic skills adults take for granted.

"There are several steps to this kind of recovery and it will take a long time," the doctors warned the family.

But, the same way she had set records on her high school's track team, Lora set records during her recuperation, skipping several of the textbook stages through which most patients proceed.

Four months after waking from her coma, the once fleet-footed track star battled to walk again.

Day after day, she made inches of progress and all the while, her tummy grew as the tiny life inside her continued to grow. Doctors could not tell Lora what effects her injuries and the medications might have had on her unborn child.

As her family prayed for her recovery, Lora prayed for her unborn child, an innocent victim of a horrible tragedy that had almost cost her her life.

The following summer, six months after the accident, Lora had recovered almost fully except for some lingering problems with peripheral vision.

That July, she gave birth to a healthy baby son.

Lynn Grisard Fullman

They call him Jonathan.
The name means "gift of God."

Delivered from the fire

Shuler Brown
Dora, Alabama

Shuler Brown woke to find smoke filling his Dora home.

He bolted to safety, but went back inside to rescue his wife and daughters.

In the confusion, he had forgotten that his family was away that night.

Within minutes of dashing back inside, Brown, overcome by smoke, passed out in the den.

Regaining consciousness, he found the

house smothered with smoke and flames and his body on fire.

Brown had no doubt then or now—he was eye to eye with death. But, the fear of dying was worse than the pain of the flames.

He knew in his heart that once he died, he would swap this fire for the fires of hell, for the way he had been living his life.

Watching as fire rained from the ceiling, he thought about his own death.

As pain riveted his body, Brown called to God, asking forgiveness for the things he had done and things he had not done.

The fear of dying left, but the agony of burning flesh remained.

Looking across the room, Brown saw a huge, white, billowing cloud.

As Brown saw the cloud drifting, he felt himself floating toward an image, a wide collection of square and rectangular boxes that appeared to be jigsawed neatly together.

The torture of burning flesh was so horrible that Brown prayed to die.

There was no hope for help. Visitors and passersby were uncommon on this dead-end road so isolated that even the garbage man did not come.

Although his upper body twisted and turned in pain, Brown, overcome by noxious gases, could not move his legs.

On that dark night, of all nights, two boys

happened up the dead end road.

Seeing the house burning and a car parked underneath, they decided to roll the car to safety. It was when they moved closer to the house that they heard Brown's cries.

The two went onto the back porch, looked inside and saw a figure covered with flames.

Unable to enter the burning house, the men screamed and jumped up and down, trying to get Brown's attention. Because of the smoke, he could not see them. But, he heard their voices and felt the thudding of their jumps.

But, still his legs wouldn't move.

As he lay dying, Brown heard a booming voice commanding, "Get up and get out of here."

His legs were still paralyzed. He could not respond.

A second time, the voice bellowed, "I said, get up and get out of here."

"When God commands you, He'll give you the strength to do what He says to do," Brown says today.

This time, on legs that minutes earlier would not move, Brown stood, went toward the noise that he heard outside and bolted through the window, plunging six feet to the ground.

His flesh still was burning.

The boys dragged Brown away from the

Lynn Grisard Fullman

house and the flames, then called for help.

Brown was taken to the hospital, but doctors predicted he would not live.

But after two and a half months in intensive care, two months in the burn unit, four and a half months in a rehabilitation hospital and forty-eight operations, Brown went home.

Later, he returned to his job at Alabama Power Company where he was a crew methods and training specialist. Almost eight years later, he took early retirement.

Brown lost his left hand, his left ear, an eyelid, the index finger on his right hand, most of his hair and most of the use of his right hand.

But, Brown does not see the losses.

"The result of that fire is the greatest thing that ever happened to me," Brown says, referring to the salvation he found on that fiery fall night in 1982.

After staring death squarely in the face, Brown is convinced of several things.

"If you reject Christ, you go to the same hell that I was breaths away from.

"God," Brown says, "is not just in the business of hearing and answering prayers - but of providing miracles."

For Brown, the miracle came in the shape of two men wandering for no apparent reason down a secluded road, a bellowing voice and a second chance at life.

A lost priest or angel of mercy

Lois Alexander
Birmingham, Alabama

Little Ron Alexander had not been riding a bicycle long when he took a nasty spill that almost cost him his life.

Peddling the quiet streets near his home, the youngster, along with his older brother and sister, may have accidentally hit a pothole. For whatever reason, the six-year-old flew over the handlebars and thudded head-first onto the pavement.

"Moooooommmmm. Daaaaaaaaaaad," the brother and sister screamed as they raced home to get help for their little brother.

Lois and Dale Alexander, sensing this was no ordinary accident, rushed to their injured son. Ron lay in a motionless heap on the street, not far from the shiny bicycle he had been so proud of.

Lois, who today lives in Birmingham and works for Automatic Food Services, scooped up her baby son as her husband ran for the car. When the rural hospital in Tracy, Minnesota realized that young Ron's injuries needed more sophisticated care than they could give, they sent the family by ambulance ninety miles to a hospital in Sioux Falls.

During the trip, the youngster three times went into convulsions. Doctors, awaiting his arrival, quickly assessed his condition, started him on anti-convulsion drugs then admitted him to the hospital.

On the fourth day, Ron was released, and his parents took him home.

"Watch him carefully," the doctors had warned as they watched Lois and Dale leaving with their son.

That afternoon, snugly back home, things began returning to normal. Dale was at work, the other children were away and Lois, at last, breathed a sigh of relief.

The calm was not to last. The day after returning home, Ron worsened. The serenity was shattered by his cries.

"Mom," the child called, "I can't see."

Lois looked into the youngster's eyes only to see them completely dilated like two huge, black saucers.

Once Lois stared into those eyes, she knew she needed help.

"Can you go with me?" she asked a neighbor who had dropped in to check on the young patient.

"I, I, I don't know," the neighbor stammered, obviously frightened by the situation.

Knowing she would have to drive her stick-shift car, Lois needed help with her son who might at any minute go into another seizure.

Not waiting for the neighbor, Lois scooped the youngster into her arms and headed out the front door, all the while wondering if she could manage the drive alone.

It was then that she saw a priest walking up the sidewalk.

"Is this the rectory?" he asked, confusing the Alexanders' house for the home of the priest who served the nearby church.

Lois never answered his question. "Father," she blurted, "I need your help. I've got to get my son to the hospital."

The priest put Lois and Ron in the front seat of his car and sped to the hospital. Nurses later would report that the priest had asked if there was anything he could do to help. And, before leaving, he had waited until Dale arrived at the hospital to be

Lynn Grisard Fullman

with his wife and son.

Once Ron was stable, the priest slipped away, and Lois never saw him again.

The youngster was treated at the rural hospital and later sent once again to Sioux Falls where doctors arrested his seizures by increasing his medications.

Before Ron's accident, the Alexanders had lived four years in their house. During that time, never once had any clergyman mistaken their home for the rectory which served the church sitting cattycornered across the street. In fact, while the house was close to the church it was not situated in such a way to be easily mistaken for the rectory.

What's more, in the six years that the Alexanders remained there, never again did a priest even walk their sidewalk in search of the rectory.

A priest had come only once.

And, that one time was the day when Lois and her son needed his help.

Epilogue

I've always believed in miracles, even though I've neither heard heavenly choirs nor come face to face with a winged angel.

But, I have sensed, I suppose, the presence of angels and have known that miracles do happen.

Although some people, at an early age, are visited by angels, I never encountered any during the years I was growing up.

From the beginning, as a baby boomer born after my father's return from his Air Force stint in World War II, my life was fairly normal. I had two parents, one brother, a black dog named Cindy and lived in a small house on a tree-lined street in Chattanooga.

The picture-perfect life was not to last.

Lynn Grisard Fullman

When I was a high school junior, my parents divorced.

Their split came a couple of years after President Kennedy had been gunned down in Dallas. As though I were tossing and turning in a cyclone, I found myself hurt, shaken, disillusioned.

Where, I wondered, were the miracles?

If angels were whispering, or softly chanting their songs, I heard nothing.

Not long after divorcing, my mother gave me her wedding ring.

"...I don't want it anymore," she had told me, and I didn't blame her.

She took the diamond-topped gold band from the back of her dresser drawer and handed it to me.

Inside the inscription¨ "JLG to MCG 3-30-40" was a constant reminder of her marriage to my father and a time when high school sweethearts had sought out a justice of the peace and had married.

They were young—too young according to their parents—but they loved each other and nothing more mattered to them.

But, by the time she gave the ring to me, their love had faded.

It didn't smite me to see and wear the ring the way it did my mother. For me, it was a reminder of the days when our family had been a family.

After she gave the band to me, I wore it next to my own wedding ring as a reminder of the family that no longer was.

Vividly, I still remember when my father packed his things and left our home.

I had heard their voices and listened to his stirrings. I knew that he was going. Before walking out the back door, he came to me in my room and feebly tried to explain.

"I'm leaving because your mother and I no longer love each other."

Looking away from him I twisted a paper clip back and forth, back and forth, until at last the metal snapped into two pieces. Tears streamed down my face. I said nothing, because there was nothing to say.

Their decision ended a 26-year marriage which had been stormy for several years.

The divorce was everything divorces are reputed to be - bitter words, hurt, strife.

Within a few years, both of my parents married others, and it seemed, from outward appearances, that life's wrinkles were smoothing out.

In time, though, Mother's husband died of a heart attack and Daddy's marriage ended in divorce. Again, they both were alone.

The miracle began when my mother phoned my brother's house and my father answered.

For the first time in 17 years, they talked.

After that, the next few weeks were a whirlwind of visits, phone calls, apologies, explanations and resolutions.

Six weeks later, as a minister married them, I slipped the ring from my finger and handed it to

Lynn Grisard Fullman

mother.

I returned the ring on March 30, the same date as the one etched in the ring—only 43 years after the first marriage.

The ring she had thought she never would want had come to mean something more.

Today, with the ring back where it belongs, my parents are quick to proclaim, "Miracles do happen."

Theirs is not the only miracle I have lived, but it is, perhaps, the one that has meant the most to me. It is the biggest and the best.

Even though I have not seen angels, I trust that they hover around me and those I love.

Even though I cannot explain miracles, I only can hope that they remain a part of all of our lives.

Alabama Miracles

Lynn Grisard Fullman

About the author

Lynn Grisard Fullman, a native of Chattanooga where she graduated from Girls' Preparatory School, in 1971 earned a degree in journalism from Samford University in Birmingham, Ala.

Ms. Fullman, whose byline has appeared in regional and national publications, has worked as a free-lance writer since 1975. She is a member of the American Society of Journalists and Authors; North American Travel Journalists; International Food, Wine and Travel Writers; and the National Federation of Press Women.

She lives in Birmingham with her husband, Milton, with whom she has two daughters, Cameron and Christine.